So Surprised to Find You Here

So Surprised to Find You Here

poems

Bart Sutter

NODIN PRESS

Cover art: Dorothea Diver
Cover photo: Larry Turbes
Cover design: John Toren
Author Photo: Cheryl Dannenbring

Library of Congress Control Number: 2022944963

9 8 7 6 5 4 3 2 1

ISBN: 978-1-947237-48-3

Published by
Nodin Press
210 Edge Place,
Minneapolis, MN 55418
www.nodinpress.com

Printed in USA

*For Cheryl Dannenbring
and Walt Prentice*

Also by Bart Sutter

Poetry
Nordic Accordion: Poems in a Scandinavian Mood
Chester Creek Ravine: Haiku
The Reindeer Camps and Other Poems
Farewell to the Starlight in Whiskey
The Book of Names: New and Selected Poems
Pine Creek Parish Hall and Other Poems
Cedarhome

Fiction
My Father's War and Other Stories

Essays
Cold Comfort: Life at the Top of the Map

Contents

VI
The Moon Beside the Canoe

VII
Coda

I

The Baba Way

Marsh Marigolds

The hiking trail takes me uphill
And then through wetlands in the woods,
The river still ahead. It's dark
In here, the water black. I slosh
Through shallow pools, rock hop,
Cross a crude boardwalk, and notice
Marigolds, marsh marigolds,
Half grown but glowing in the dusk,
Their cup-shaped, deep green leaves
Still small, their yellow flowers
Still more bud than bloom, and think
Of country girls with whom I went
To grade school way back when.
Jeanie, Sandy, Margie, Joyce . . .
I'm so surprised to find you here,
Half hidden in the cedar shade,
And after all these years.

Harlow Told Me No

I remember him, eleven, with a shining pompadour
As foolish as his father's. A chubby guy,
But could he hit! And run? I can see him now,
His hairdo like a headdress, that mesmerizing squint
Before the windup and the pitch. He could throw
A sinker like a rock. His dad had taught him how,
And it was frightening. Harlow didn't talk a lot.
His mother, dark and quiet, Chippewa,
May have been responsible for that, but I
Remember how she chuckled to the chickens,
Fanning out the yellow grain, yelling at the geese.

They had a couple acres, sheep and goats, a horse.
Nothing but a basement until they built the house.
Harlow's father built it. Harlow's father owned
A lever-action Winchester that spoke
In sophisticated whispers and a complicated click,
And other guns, and fishing rods, interesting
Minnow nets and spears. I remember snowshoes.
Harlow's father trapped for mink for miles
Down the river. Harlow got to go.

Harlow loved the races. I did, too. Somehow
They embodied our ambition to be men, like the drivers
Strapped inside their stock-cars, jostling for position
Like a herd of crazy cattle crowding through the gate.
Blue sparks, engine flames, the stink of gasoline,

The blather and the racket reminded us of something,
Something, something more important
     than the checkered flag of victory.

But Harlow's father had a heart attack.
He died. There was nothing you could say,
And Harlow didn't talk much. Not long after that,
My dad and I invited Harlow to the races.
I remember how I asked him in his bedroom,
Permeated by the odor of that sickly sweet pomade
With which he greased his hair. I remember
Pictures taped up on the walls, pictures everywhere,
Cars cut out of magazines, cars that he had drawn,
But though I asked him carefully,
Harlow wouldn't go. He simply would not budge.
Nothing you could say. Harlow told me, "No."

Single Wing

My god, but I loved football, even when
We were being beaten by a bunch of bruisers,
Even when Coach paired me off with Nannenga,
Thinking it might do me good to bang
Our largest lineman in a blocking drill,
And Nannygoat, our heavyweight, just laughed
And barely budged, although I threw myself
At him till I was almost sobbing with
Frustration and fatigue. Yes, even then.
I loved putting on my thigh and shoulder pads
Like armor and walking to the practice field,
And maybe most of all—crossing the street,
My helmet in my hand—the clatter of my cleats.

Oddly, though, what I remember best
Came that afternoon when Coach decided,
Since we'd lost a couple games by awful scores,
That we should resurrect an old formation
From the 1940s, the Single Wing,
On the theory if you can't win with brawn
You might bewilder them with weirdness.
The Single Wing—outdated—was new to us.
We ran some plays against the junior team—
Some dives, a crossbuck that I loved, a sweep—
And then, returning to the huddle, noticed
A flight of gulls, ring-bills, flashing
Overhead, headed south, gilded

By the sinking sun. And they were only
Scouts, succeeded by long lines
That stretched across the sky. "Huddle up!"
We heard Coach holler, and we did, then spread
In our formation, yet nobody got set.
All of us were looking up, up,
Our footsteps wandering as if we'd been
Concussed, gazing, all agog and dazzled by
The flood of ghostly birds that filled the sky,
Flying silently, relentlessly,
White bodies tinted gold. Even Coach.
And even then I thought, "I think I will
Remember this even when I'm old."
Now I am old, and it's as I foretold.

The last gulls left the sky, and Coach,
Who always looked as if he'd like to be
Biting a cigar, smiled all around
And growled, "All right, you knot-heads,
Back to work." Hargis called the sweep.
We took our places: Bow-legged Murphy,
Tailback, to my left, Danny crouched
Behind the line. "Down, ready, set.
Hut two, hut two!" Danny sealed the end,
I raced past and smacked the linebacker,
And Murphy, who could fly, flew.

The Baba Way

I am seventy, Otto is six months,
And yet he sits there in his Bumbo
Like an infant king, while we are ranged
Along the long pine table, his courtiers.
Otto's mother, incidentally our daughter,
Serves him bits of grown-up food,
To which the boy responds with glee,
Although he only has two teeth.
Otto's otherwise first-rate father
Has this weakness: he cannot bear
To witness the battlefield his child makes
Of pudgy flesh and Bumbo tray:
Strawberry smears across his cheek,
Apple sauce hair, beet bits leaking blood
All down his front, the gore, the crumbs,
Food scraps scattered everywhere.

And yet we all feel elevated by
The joy with which this small boy eats.
He gums a bite, saliva drips, he swallows,
Smiles, reaches for the heavens with both hands,
And hollers, "Allah!" releasing laughter
Like the clamor of church bells at a wedding
Or a coronation, which we join.
My goodness, I'm thinking, this
White German-American baby
Must be Muslim. Yet once the laughter

Of his subjects has subsided, Otto
Ingests a golden gobbet of squash, then
Reaches for the skies again, proclaiming,
"Baba!" And I see that I misheard the first time:
Not "Allah!" but "Baba!" Or was it "Abba!"
The Aramaic word that Christ is said
To have pronounced, crying for his Father
From the cross. But Otto is not suffering.
No, no. This is joy, as pure and plain
As the potato lump that Otto squishes
In his fist and feeds himself. "Baba!"
Definitely "Baba!" So the boy is Hindu
Or Sufi, maybe. Whatever his religion,
I repent my daily puling and complaining,
Wonderstruck that I'd forgot
The sunlight in the orange, the honeycomb
Of bread, the nectar that is milk.

There's a gap in the laughter of my tablemates
As they turn their looks on me to see
Tears trembling in my eyelashes
And drip, drip-dropping on my plate.
Then all of us are laughing—yes, me, too—
Because I've been converted to
The Way of Food and Gratitude,
The Way of Baba, transported
Into the Kingdom of Gladness,
Where I intend to live forever.

Thea Sofia Beneath the Piano

Little Drummer Girl, Table Smacker, Two-Fisted Pounder
Of your high-chair tray, Whacker of Wooden Spoons
On the hardwood floor, or, should nothing else
Come to hand, Slapper of Your Own Small Self, you
Invoke the music of the galaxies when you bang
The living drum beneath your own breastbone.
Play on, play on.

Town Crier, Crib Crooner, Self-Singer
Of Dada and Lazy-ass Vowels in your dusky room,
Reveller in Reveille at bedtime or midnight or three a.m.,
You-*can*-get-us-up, you-*can*-get-us-up, you-*can*-get-us-up
In the morning or anytime whatsoever you please
With your lonesome yodels and siren songs.
Sing on, sing on.

Mistress of the One-armed Commando Crawl, Scooter
Across Smooth Floors, you find yourself gazing up
At the bottom side of the baby grand your mother's
Mother inherited from *her* mom, as if at the depths
     of the sky,
Bug-eyed with Wonder and Wow at the sound.
Ten-fingered Fairy, when we are all gone,
Play on, play on.

Good to Have a Brother

It's good to have a brother who, when he tips the canoe,
And you wallow around waist-deep in the river,
Furious and firing sopping wet gear at his head,
Who, even as you thrash and flail and swear,
Stands there on the riverbank, soaked through,
Laughing at your anger until you're laughing, too.

It's good to have a brother who, when you've
Been cooped up in the car too long
And he praises recent action by his church
And you sniff, announcing how you think the world
Is waiting for a new religion, tells you, sharply,
"Well, then, you better get busy." You spew
Your coffee, and he starts laughing, too.

So Long, Tom

My friend had lost his cowboy hat
But wore his blue jean jacket still,
Stumped the floor with a chalk-white cane,
Eased his body down, and sat,
Wheezing as if he'd climbed a hill.
He shrugged off pain, slowly explained
How I'd have to shout for him to hear.
Appalled, I hollered about that year
We paddled and portaged to Raven Lake.
He said he thought it would likely take
About a month to set things right,
Then he'd go without a fight.
I touched his face and yelled goodbye.
His eyes were targets, blue bull's-eyes.

The Hand

Some men have a steadiness,
An easy way, a readiness
To listen to your dreams and grief,
Raw resentment, tangled plans,
Then clarify and deepen your belief.
What great good luck to find you such a man.

Within that man, however young,
A *gubbe* tends a kettle hung
Among the melting drifts of snow
And leafless trees of early spring.
He keeps his crackling fire low,
His blackened kettle bubbling.

Mumbling around the fire,
He throws in snow to cool desire,
Cedar fronds to freshen you,
Sap drawn from his maple stand.
You take encouragement from such a brew
And, on your shoulder, feel his hand.

In memoriam: Bill Beyer

[*gubbe*: Swedish for old man]

When I Remember Donny

I like to recall the waterfall
When he was just back from Nam
And he found us there where Kennedy Creek
Drops fifty feet to the pebble beach
On the shore of Lake Superior.
We'd clamber down with a rope
To camp in the open air.
The beach had bluffs for bookends,
So it was an island, too,
One of our loved retreats.

October. Golden leaves. And cold.
Donny'd been up to Mirror Lake,
Our favorite hideaway. He'd
Sneaked across to Canada
And portaged in to find
The perfect middle of nowhere.
Escaping there through memory
Had gotten him through his tour,
But now the trapper's shack was real,
The jack pines, birch, the silver lake
Dimpling with rain, which turned to snow,
Then snow geese by the hundreds
Flooding overhead so that he shouted
Gladness, thanks, and awe.

Donny was ecstatic now, recounting this
And how, as he'd worked his way back out,
He'd encountered Charlie Cook, himself,

The rumor who'd built the shack,
Half Chippewa, and real as rock,
Standing by the beaver pond.
Charlie had his dog along,
Canoe stacked high with gear and traps.
Don confessed he'd used the shack
But left behind a fifth of scotch
Cached in the tin wood stove.
Charlie slowly smiled and said,
"You use the cabin anytime.
Anyone bother you, you tell 'em,
Charlie Cook say you stay."

We stretched out by the fire
And slipped away to sleep, lulled
By the curl of collapsing waves,
The rattle of little stones,
And the waterfall, the waterfall,
The water fell beside us there,
Our liquid hourglass. Then woke
In the dark to sizzle and sparks.
Donny had stoked the fire, sliced
Every onion from the sack
And hunched there in his peacoat,
Stirring his fricassee.
We all had a taste of the silver O's,
Buttery, spicy, sweet,
But Don ate half the pan, and
That's how he comes back to me—
Fire-lit, the backdrop dark,
Chuckling maniacally.

I hate to think how things went wrong,
Though his work on the power lines
Had juiced his bank accounts
So he could build, as time ran on,
His paradise—a garden
Big as a football field,
Pickup, Bobcat, guns, canoes.
Good women came and went, and he
Got lost, somehow, and mean.
With all he needed rigged in place,
He chose to sit in his garage
And raise a glass to nothing.
No escape from that.

I hate to think how hard his twin
Tried to call him back, mowed
His lawn, tilled his garden, called
And called and called. No answer.
Nasty rants at best. Then came the day
His twin walked in to find the corpse
Bled out, sat down, and shook.

When I learned that Don was dead,
I heard the waterfall and saw
That young man, fire-flushed,
The night so large, and a voice
Called out, "Hey, Don?
Charlie Cook say you stay."
But he was gone.

Three Big Rocks

1.

I'm no geologist,
But I do like a good-sized rock.
Fishing the Cloquet the other day,
Catching nothing but snags,
I followed a trail other feet had worn
In the grass along the riverbank,
Casting as I went. A nasty business.
The river was chockfull of rocks,
So I kept on till the faint path petered out,
Beyond where I had ever been.
The bank was bouldery now,
Black rocks big as dinosaur eggs.
When the going grew too scary,
I girded my loins, as the Bible
Seems to recommend,
Plunged off in the woods,
And fought the thorny brush.

Bless me, breaking through,
I found the water smooth, and,
At the river's edge, a rock
The size of a compact car.

Clambering onto this platform,
I stood, though it slanted riverward,
And, casting out midstream, struck

A hole two boxcars long, where,
If I could drop my bait in there,
A heavy pull came every couple casts
And a consequent tussle with thrashing
And hauling and sometimes a leap and a splash.
Over two hours, I pulled in sixteen
Fish: golden walleyes, emerald pike,
The pewter of rock bass,
Smallmouth in their scales of bronze.

I kept the largest and let the rest go.
This was a location to remember, so I christened
My discovery on the spot, pronouncing it
        The Big Rock.

            2.
The first time I saw Sweden,
My cousin showed my wife and me
Broad blue rushing rivers,
The lake where church boats race,
The cabins of my ancestors,
The church where, once upon a time,
My great-grandfather led the hymns
With a one-string instrument.
She pointed out the pasture camps
Hidden in the hills, where women herded cows
For centuries, their wild songs drifting down the slopes.
And down we went, in slickers and hard hats,
In the famous Falun copper mine.
We got an eyeful, that's for sure, but

Driving back from one of our forays,
She grinned and said, "Let's have a look at this."

The sign read, "*Stora Sten.*"
Sten, we knew, meant rock or stone,
But *stor* could mean a dozen things:
Distinguished, great, funny, wide,
Delightful, lovely, big . . . My cousin
Would not translate, but led us on
A path into the dusky woods,
Which darkened as we walked
The winding trail through spruce trees
Crowding close. But then there came
A kind of opening, and there it loomed:
The *Stora Sten*, a rough gray block of granite
Five times taller than we stood,
The size of a chapel, say, although
It had no windows. What a thing to see
Out here in all these trees, surrounding it
Like soldiers in dark uniforms. It looked
Like something you could pray to,
Your forehead pressed against its mossy side,
And so we gave it several minutes of respect.
Yet it was just absurd, some kind of
Joke the gods had dropped out of the sky.
We gazed, then met each other's eyes,
Exploding into laughter,
Although we did not speak
As we felt our way back to the car.
On our way home, our talk kept flashing

With two words that signified the mystery
We'd witnessed: *stora sten*—great big rock,
Lovely rock, delightful rock, distinguished rock—
    Stora Sten.

    3.

Up along the Manitoba border,
Where the land lies flat as slate,
The fields grow green with hay,
Cerulean with flax, glorious
With sunflowers. Yet
Winter's never far away.
Blizzards blast that place.

The wide sky is pierced by the spire
Of Pine Creek Lutheran Church,
Like a rocket on its launching pad.
I was raised here, and that steeple
Always moves me as it lifts,
A sword against the sky.

Reading in the memory book
Of that dwindling congregation,
I was struck by a woman who,
Though she loved that isolated church,
Declared her fondest recollections
Involved those times the parish met
At The Big Stone in the clearing
In the jack pines by The Bog.

I, myself, was never there,
But I can see it. I've seen photos:
Pale gray granite, ten feet high,
Its edges rounded off, about
The size of a pickup truck.

I know just enough geology
To understand such rocks are called
Erratics, having been transported
So far from their origins
Upon the backs of glaciers
And left lying, willy-nilly,
On such plains as this one,
Where the prairie meets the pines.
And I know humans just enough
To understand we're drawn to them,
Though not exactly why.

These people were erratics, too,
Carried far from Iceland, Norway,
Sweden, Denmark, with names
Like Lislegaard and Nordvall,
Dropping here, as they will say,
"Way up north of nowhere."

Gazing at their old snapshots,
My mind makes movies, and in this one,
They've already held a service
Where the pastor offered up a prayer,
Giving thanks for this fine day.

They've sung some favorite hymns—
"Rock of Ages," maybe, or
"The Church's One Foundation."
Now, though, they sing,
"Be present at our table, Lord,"
Although there is no table, but there is
This one gigantic rock, from which
No one will stray too far.

The women, wearing dresses,
Naturally, and quite a few in hats,
Display the offerings they've brought—
Chicken, hot dish, salads, pie—
And call the children off the summit of the stone.
The men, in darker clothes, cloth caps, fedoras,
Lean against the rock, and several smoke.
These people all are sinners, and they know it.
Helga envies Jennie's looks, and Arvid wouldn't mind
Helping Severt lose a tooth or two some Saturday in town,
But this is Sunday, they are neighbors, so they get along,
Gathered round this lodestone which attracted them.

I love to hear their talk, although it's blurred,
But just the buzz, the hum, the lilt, the lovely laughter.
They don't yet understand how many of their children
Will be drained away by cities, nor do they know
The creamery will close, the general store, the school,
The post office, their neighbors grow more distant,
But all the grown-ups recognize that life's a shining thing,
However hard, and somehow, somewhere, someday

They will die, and they feel somewhat less alone
By sitting, standing, kneeling here beside
     The Big Stone.

After Forty Years, Steve Luxton, Poet of the Eastern Townships, Comes to Visit, and We Talk Nonstop for Days

Vs of geese crisscross the clouds
As I tear out the garden fence
And you wing east towards Montreal.
What a wave, what a flood,
What a waterfall of talk
We tumbled under after forty
Years apart: women lost
And won, books and books and books,
The moose head on your cabin wall,
Blue lakes we've loved, and rivers run.
We spoke of many things: of Buddhists
And Republicans, of Marx, and Jesus, too,
Of friends and traitors, stratagems
For fame, the fish that got away.

We drifted on a hillside lake
And yammered in that theatre
Of autumn trees, old poets
Hard of hearing, strong of throat,
Whose blab and jabber drove the splake
Streaking toward the bottom. When
You left, you left behind such gifts:
A string-bound Chinese notebook and
A square brass box for ink,

Both inscribed with language from
Another, distant world.

What a crime to spend our lives
A thousand miles apart! My house
Has fallen silent now, but still
I hear faint echoes of electric
Talk and wonder, like a kid
Who braves the darkened hallway, drawn
By loud palaver of the grown-ups
In the glaring living room,
Or smile, as a mother might
Who overhears her boys at play.

Let's migrate like the wild birds
Between Quebec and here and back.
Let's paddle, fish, and hike the hills,
As talkative as aspen leaves,
Until one sinks into the earth
And leaves the other on his own,
Stretched out beside the fire, watching
As the embers flare, then dwindle
Till the last blue light winks out.

Their Table Prayer

Sometimes now they just hold hands
And lean toward one another,
Drifting loons on evening water,
Quiet as the dark descends.

II
Beds for the Homeless

I Was Downtown, Fingering
My Worry Beads

Of self-pity, envy, and half-cracked plans,
　　　when I noticed a man
My age with a cane, limping through the crosswalk,
And then, as if I needed the point driven home,
A second man, in a second crosswalk, at the very
　　　same time,
With neat gray beard and hair, shuffling his wheelchair
　　　along with his feet,
His arms around two canes, plus a heap of other stuff,
And a voice inside my head said, "Shame on you,
　　　Barton. Shame."

Daylilies

What kind of music issues
From the brilliant trumpets
Of the daylilies? Is it pitched
So high only dogs can hear?
Birds? Butterflies? Bees?

Are these colorful megaphones
Howling like storm sirens
At the beetles and ants? *Take cover!*
Head for the cellar! Immediately!
No. Nothing so lovely—
Deep orange, buttercream—
Would sound so alarming.

We humans may not hear
The music of these tender trumpets,
But who can deny that we feel it,
A *basso profundo* so low
It makes everything tremble
Yet steadies us, too, like the ultrasound
From those long Buddhist horns in Tibet,
Rising right out of the bedrock.

Who wrote this music? Who knows?
All I know is that walking past
Our floral orchestra, I feel calmer
And friendly toward my neighbors,
Even the ones who annoy me!

Beds for the Homeless

We pulled the nails from painted wood
And planed it so the grain looked good,

Glued the Douglas fir and pine,
Clamped the pieces over time

Till they had set, and we could cut
Headboards, legs, and sides to fit.

As we bent to putty holes,
With pampered bodies, troubled souls,

We bowed our heads, as if in prayer,
While saws and joiners tore the air.

Routers carved a fine design
In headboards, keeping you in mind

And how the hover of a dove
Might bless your rest, your making love,

Easing children off to sleep,
Breathing slowly, dreaming deep.

These beds now number sixty-nine:
Two thousand hours of our time.

A land where families freeze in cars
Has wished upon some evil star.

Our sleep is fitful, peace is marred,
Considering this nation's ours.

May these beds support your health.
Forgive us for our luck and wealth.

Eighteen Pairs of Mittens Plus One

Alice's place was a cozy catastrophe.
"What should we work on today?" Bev asked.
"Well," said Alice, "I suppose we could start
With my mitten drawer over there by the door."

Alice, at eighty-eight, was still vivacious,
Although she'd grown wobbly these last few years
And also half blind. It would not be too much to say
That Bev, some twenty years younger, loved her.

Bev tugged hard on the mitten drawer,
But it would not come, seemed to be stuck,
Then shot free, and a couple of balled-up
Mitten pairs popped out onto the floor—

Like a jack-in-the-box but less fun.
Bev removed the drawer and dumped
The whole load of mitten-balls on the bed.
There were eighteen pairs plus one blue singleton.

"That's a lot of mittens, Alice," said Bev.
"I need a lot. I'm always losing them."
"Could we aim to get rid of half?
We could start with this blue orphan."

"That one's practically new." "Where's the mate?"
"I've been waiting for it to turn up."

"How long?" "A year . . . maybe more."
"Sorry, Alice, this one's a goner."

"I could use it as a hot pad."
Bev gave her a grave look. "You've got hot pads."
"Well, okay, but it doesn't seem right." Bev
Dropped the lonesome mitten in a grocery bag.

And then unwrapped one fist-sized bundle
After another till thirty-six mittens lay on the bed
Like the raised hands of an entire platoon
Volunteering for dangerous duty.

"These are badly stained," said Bev
And dangled a pair close enough
That Alice could see for herself.
"Still warm," the old woman said.

"But you can't ask a stranger
To wear soiled things, and you've got better
By far." So the mitten dialogue went,
Not without laughter, as Bev donned a pair

To improvise a puppet show
Or clapped them over her ears
To shut out Alice's argument.
At last their medieval debate

Grew downright metaphysical.
"This one's got a hole," Bev said.

"That's not really a hole." "Alice,"
Bev said, thrusting one finger through

And wagging it in front of her face,
"Alice, that's a hole." "But it can be mended."
 "Are you going to mend it?" "Someday, maybe."
"Do you expect me to mend it?" "No."

"Then into the bag it goes. And now let's have tea."
This happy ending carries conflicting morals:
Good people may still need a shove,
And patience is a form of love.

The Tin Can Man

When I was young, I knew someone
Who lived part-time in an iron lung.
I'd say he was late thirties then,
And my parents were kind of in love with him.
His name was Harold, same as my dad's,
And I was told the two of them had
Made friends while at the seminary.
Yes, this Harold was a pastor.
How could he be if he
Lived in an iron lung, you ask.

He had an oxygen tank and mask
For emergencies and only used
The lung at night plus an hour or two
Bad afternoons. Otherwise,
Harold stabilized his wobbly
Walk with crutch or cane.
It was polio, you know, the bane
Of a generation then.

                    But when
We visited, our family witnessed
A relatively normal life. Eunice,
A vivid redhead, had been his nurse,
Still was, but also now his laughing wife.
That parsonage felt free of grief;
The major tone, instead, was joy,
And, though I was just a four-foot boy,

Harold asked inviting questions
Without one hint of condescension.

We went next door to hear him preach.
You could have heard a church mouse squeak
As Harold conveyed his sermon,
Which sounded casual as conversation.
How he held that small-town parish!
It was plain how much they cherished
This damaged man who hung suspended
In their pulpit. When the service ended,
All eyes followed as he swayed and swung
On crutches down the aisle while they sang,
Then filed out to shake the hand that wasn't leaning
Hard, hard on his left crutch; and all of this had meaning.

After church, Eunice served a generous meal
With laughter and light-hearted talk
Until she noticed Harold was going pale.
She stood. A gentle shock
Ran through the room as she announced
That it was time for Harold's treatment.
Her husband struggled up at once.
We stood, too, and made an easement,
Moving chairs out of his way
As he swung past, assuring us he'd be okay.
Eunice stood beside the door
Of a room that they'd kept closed before.
"Just give us a couple of minutes.
Then feel free to come and visit."

My parents cleared the dishes and prepared me
For what we were about to see,
Which proved both interesting and scary.
The iron lung appeared to fill the room,
A shining cylinder of steel
Resting on its side. Its motor thrummed
And purred, so all of us could feel it
Working, and we also heard it wheeze,
Releasing pressure, helping Harold breathe.
And there was Harold, just his head
Exposed, the rest of him inside.
I was horrified but almost laughed:
He looked stuck inside a can!
And yet he seemed entirely relaxed.
Therefore, we sat with him, the tin can man.
The grownups talked a good long while,
And I still see that pastor's smile,
Pearly skin, black wavy hair,
And those blue eyes, which tantalized
So somehow I'm still sitting there.

I wish I had a photograph
That could show you Harold's aura.
The Tin Can Man was radiant.
And though I could not guess
            just what that meant,
I felt I might remember him forever,
And, turns out, I have.

Firearms and Backhoe

Although the sky and sea were bright
    with waterfowl below,
The birdwatchers decided not to walk
    beyond the sign
Declaring: "Warning I Own Both Firearms
    and Backhoe."

It seemed a joke—or half a joke—but then
    you never know
Who's cracking wise or mad enough
    to cross what line,
And weren't there other spots to view
    the waterfowl below?

They stood there reading and re-reading
    for a while, though,
Smiling, musing, shaking their heads,
    still not quite resigned
To such unfriendly words: "I Own Both Firearms
    and Backhoe."

In Sweden, they'd have had every legal right to go
Across this land, pick berries, even camp,
    with no designs
Except to marvel at the million waterfowl below.

This wasn't Sweden. This was somewhere else, and woe
To those who doubted anyone should own a coastline
Or those who couldn't read "I Own
           Both Firearms and Backhoe."

It mattered not one whit that their intentions
           were benign.
The sign declared the land, the sky, the sea—*all mine!*
Although the sky and sea were glimmering
           with waterfowl below,
The sign said: "Warning I Own Both Firearms
           and Backhoe."

Large and Difficult Trees

for John Sigurdson

This was a difficult tree, tall and twisty.
I didn't like the looks of it—corkscrew ugly—
But a job's a job, I thought. Normally I work alone,
But I brought a helper for this one,
A ground man for my safety line.

Can you believe this? The customer told me,
Head cocked, squinting at the tiptop,
"I'm glad we've got your business card
So we'll know which hospital to send you to."
Then he laughed and turned back toward the house.
I'm going up sixty feet, and you tell me
        something like that?

The fear is always there, but you control it.
You trust your techniques, your gear. You check,
Double-check. And then I've been at this
An awful long time. I've got my spikes,
My harness, I get a highline up there,
And here I had a helper on the ground.
With the spikes I go right up, a human fly.

I've got my saw on the belt rope, so I yank
That up as needed, lopping limbs,
And she's going all right, considering
The ugly torque in the trunk and the spring

In a couple of danglers. I'm skyhigh now,
And that's when I see the hive, far out
On a crookedy limb with a twist up close.
That hive hung down like a fat handbag.

It's not like I never encountered a hive before,
So I didn't overthink it, but that was a kinky limb,
And it took too long to cut. Finally, she fell,
And I moved on. A little later, I look down
And see, from where I've dropped my limbs,
A swirl of smoke is rising. I'm thinking, *What?*
Turns out they were African killer bees.
They've been moving into our area. These
Knew exactly who I was and just what I had done.

They were on my head like a helmet.
The buzzing is horrific. And then they start to sting.
It's like you're doused in gasoline,
And somebody struck a match. I've got
My highline. I can rappel. So I unhook,
But the panic! I'm jouncing down, but then
The line gets caught, so I have to climb back up
To work it loose! *Where's my ground man?*
He's been attacked, himself, and run.

Finally I'm down, stretched out, feeling
I might be done. The bees are on me still.
I crawl and somehow find a faucet, blast
Cold water all over my head, then lie out flat
And wait to see if my throat will close

Or I'll get to go on breathing.
They must have had an allergy in that family
Because the wife runs out with an epi pen.
Probably saved my life. When they turned me loose
From the hospital, I looked like I had gone
Eighteen rounds, demolished by a bruiser.

It's funny how life goes. I started in tree service
When I was just a kid, but I tried out different things.
In my zigzag way, I even earned, eventually,
My university degree. But I always came back to this.
I've spent a good share of my life in the sky.
I'm sixty now, self-employed, no pension anywhere.
I'm stuck. I'll have to work until I die, but
        in these latter days
I do my best to stay away
        from large and difficult trees.

Louise

My boyhood rang the other day,
A phone call from Bill Brass,
Who lived just up the hill
In our village of Blink-and-Miss-It
On the banks of the Long Gone River.

We hadn't spoken in years, and so
It was dreamy to reminisce
About biking miles along dirt roads,
All but drowning in gravel pit ponds,
Smoking ourselves round fires
We lit like junior arsonists.

Bill told me how his father died, how
His mother hung on in a nursing home.
Louise. She of the coppery hair,
As if her head were on fire. Must have been
In her thirties then, she of the tart remark
And that fabulous, free laughter.
She could cut you in half with a phrase.
Louise loved music and played
The piano and organ at church
With accurate passion. It was always
Easter with her somehow. Please rise.
And she was rising. Hallelujah!

I resurrect that afternoon
We kids were running around
Our yard, and Louise dropped by
To check on hers. I was ten? Eleven?
Louise was wearing a scoop-neck dress,
And when she bent to tuck in the shirt
Of one of her small boys, I looked
Right down her dress at paradise.
Well, I was standing right in front of her!
Lush breasts. My torso flushed with warmth,
My chest expanded. She straightened
And met my eyes. I blushed but felt
Forgiven, too, and my flesh knew
It was going to be grand to be a grown-up.
Three to five seconds I have remembered
For sixty years. Her dress was a cotton print,
Butter cream with cherries bright as blood.

Bill told me Louise has gone blind
But keeps a piano in her room,
And, though she can't see to read music,
Still has the old hymns by heart.
Hallelujah, anyhow, Louise, my love,
My flag and emblem of womanhood.

Bill's a good son. He calls his mother daily.
When he dares to ask her, "How's your health?"
She answers, characteristically,
"Better than I'd like it to be."

Lost Locations

What happened to Norland, Grit, Pomme de Terre?
Once bustling towns, they're neither here nor there.
It upsets me when these days nobody talks
About berries near Pinecreek, Duxby, or Fox.
As a boy, I thought those hamlets would last forever.
It seems they've all gone the way of Belle River.
The ore was mined. The forest logged. Its function
Lost when the railway died, there went
      Winnipeg Junction.
What about Old Crow Wing, Mallard, and Moose,
Where people sold grog and used to chew snoose?
What happened to Darling, Dorothy, Hazel, Duane?
They had no importance. I miss them, just the same.
I do, and assume you do, too, though not many will,
Bewildered, keep asking the way to Gravelville
Or wonder out loud in the woods around Faunce,
"Where did they go? I heard how people
      lived here once."

Big Ideas

All my life long I've gotten lost
In the sensuous rush of pussy willows
And women's breasts, the gurgle
Of trout streams and babies. But
What's it all mean? Where's the wisdom?
Now I'm in my sixties, now's the time
For grand abstraction, authoritative
Statement, the very royal "We."

Come on, old boy. We want
The sort of thing a reader underlines
And writes beside: *How true!*
Okay, then. When in the course
Of worldwide events . . . Threescore
And several years ago . . . Life
Death doth end and each night . . .

It's no use. I took a walk today,
And big ideas kept escaping me
Like deer that flash white flags
And flee. The truth is that the most
Important thing I know right now
Is how the long, dead grasses look
So blonde against the snow.

III

I'd Like to Sleep Like the Seals on the Beach at Point Lobos

The Kelp at San Simeon

for Bettina

I hadn't seen the Pacific in sixty years, but it's still here!
The wind sings, the sky is pearly gray, cashmere.
We look and look. We wander the beach,
          examining this
And that, intent but quick, like skittery shorebirds.

Here are some tangles of kelp I must heft. Weighty
As buckets of water. Electrical nightmares,
Wires crossed and intertwined, impossible to sort out,
Like Christmas lights back home. When you walk
On a carpet of kelp, the bulbs pop underfoot.

These deteriorating baskets have been well brined
But will turn to dirt anyhow, as the Irish knew,
Who hauled heavy loads of sea drapes
Up cliffs, year after year after year,
Till kelp and rock became sweet grassy fields.

It's the holidays somehow, the gifts have been opened,
The wrapping unfurled in windrows around us.
We throw our hands in the air, we laugh, we shout,
We sing to our savior, the sea.

I'd Like to Sleep Like the Seals
on the Beach at Point Lobos

Who lie around like so many logs that have drifted
      here from Japan.
The long voyage has stripped off their bark,
      worn away worries,
They're down to satiny skin. Must be nice
      to lie around naked.
We don't do that a lot where I'm from. We peer
      down at the cove,
Our nerves sparkle and glint with delight.
      What luck to share the planet
With undulant swimmers, practiced professional
      nappers like these,
Who roll themselves over like logs, suddenly,
      and sometimes applaud
In their sleep. Oh, teach us to praise this water,
      this earth,
This lucky, lucky life! The yearling turns
      his face to us,
Eyes closed, he has whiskers already,
      he makes his face
To shine upon us, the face of an ancient
      Chinese sage.

The Waves Come Flying Here
All the Way from Hawaii

They curl and collapse, they fountain and foam like
      champagne,
They geyser and shatter in spatters of spray.
And why not? They've been gone a long time.
      Why not
Celebrate? The surf scoters sink out of sight
      in a trough,
Then suddenly rise on a swell to glide
      the watery avalanche.
They concentrate on their calling, along for the ride
      but undistracted
By seething and swelling rebellions, pointless
      pandemonium.
Their brethren, the white-winged scoters,
      drown in the drink
But rise resurrected, just as expected, calm
      and completely at home.

Truchas

Albuquerque grows like a gargantuan amoeba,
Santa Fe becomes a cartoon of itself,
Taos takes on the charm of a traffic jam;
But here in the high, dry air of Truchas,
Perfumed by juniper, piñon, and sage,
Nothing much happens this morning: the road
Runs right to the edge and then has second thoughts,
Turns off, descends in lazy loops to desert floor.
The log-and-mud huts of the last hundred years
Slump slowly toward the abyss. The cliff
Slides away in one long, vertiginous swoop
To the blue-black Jemez Mountains, oceanic
Waves of stone that will not curl or break.

Here is the blessed boredom
we traveled a thousand miles to find.

Two horses, elegant as girls in formal gowns,
Sashay casually and bow down to the grass.
Crickets creak in their forests of clover.
A hummingbird buzzes by. Somebody's goose
Announces herself with a rusty honk,
And a rooster shouts hip-hip-hooray.
The light is clear and clean. A spicy breeze
Rattles the cottonwood leaves, but the bell
On the tin-roofed chapel remains becalmed,
Still as steel, silent as a mountain saint.

Cliff swallows chitter and sew up the sky,
Sail home to the small adobe house
They've daubed above the casita door.

Roadrunner

We looked for you for miles
Along the Arizona highways
While vultures kited overhead,
Sparrows scattered, ravens
Stuck like crosses to the sky.
We were warned that "Dust Storms
May Exist" but saw no sign
Of you, the goonybird.
Then, pop! Surprise! You
Hopped atop a compost pile
In the corner of a Tucson parking lot,
Bouncing this way, jouncing that,
Then pulled your disappearing act

And, presto-change-o, showed up
On the pavement in New Mexico,
Breaking through some tangled scrub,
Bursting into open field, and sailed away
On stubby wings to safety in the dust.

Trickster, cartoon, goofball bird,
Knee-high, feathered dinosaur
With wings that barely work,
I croak these words in praise of you
For getting by on mice and bugs,
Birds and lizards, spiders, snakes.
Yes! You can snatch yourself a rattler

And whip-crack his head on a rock,
Then swallow him whole or, if need be,
Never mind if his tail still sticks out of your beak.

Who isn't pleased with the way you live
Up to your name? That morning
In the Mimbres Valley you shot up
The asphalt ahead of me, then
Veered off, so I stopped to watch
You gallop away up the two-track,
A gangly girl with a Mohawk,
Who threw me a burglar's glance
Before you ducked into the brush.

Roadrunner, roadrunner,
Illiterate, masked *bandito*,
Your toes print exes in the dust,
Make your mark repeatedly,
Reminding us how we are new,
And all these cacti, rocks, and sunburned sand
Have long belonged to you.

Why Swedes Are So Stiff

When rains drenched the fields
And the crops all failed,
Winter came on anyway,
Winter kept coming, and stayed.
We ate the potatoes, we slaughtered the sow,
We devoured the bread, we butchered the cow.
We had no wheat, we had no rye,
It was clear the children were going to die.
Our prayers to Jesus did no good.
At last we got up off our knees
And asked the forest gods for food.
Desperate, fugitive, shy, ashamed,
We stripped the rough bark off the trees,
Peeled away the sweet membrane,
Ground it into fragrant dust,
Then baked and ate that dry breadstuff.
It's true. In those days we ate wood.
And though we often wish we could
Be more spontaneous, loud, and bright—
At least less cautious, less uptight—
We still have that stiffness in us.
We have to ask you to forgive us.

Italian River Houses

"Many Italians have river houses,"
The voice of my dream declared.
The voice of a god or the narrator
Of a documentary, it spoke
With so much authority, I believed.
I would have gladly gone out with him
For a beer, even though I can't drink anymore—
Or a glass of wine, red wine,
A deep dark bottomless red.

"Many Italians have river houses,"
The man announced with such confidence
You could tell he had been there,
Traveled that sun-spangled country
And read all about it, and not just the internet, either,
But books, real books, real actual books,
Remember them?

Many Italians have river houses, I guess
Because they're so squished inside
Their apartments, and they want to get down
By the river. Who doesn't? Only those
Who are already dead inside and afraid
Of a couple of bugs. Who cares? Ever hear
Of a fly swatter? Jeez. I could see them,
These Italians. Okay, one. I could see this one
Italian. He wore a striped shirt, a straw hat,

A black mustache, and a smile. He was happy
Down there at his river house.

I couldn't see any women, though I knew
They swaggered nearby, women
Who looked like Sophia Loren,
The most gorgeous in history
(Aside from my wife, of course), but
Old and young, in every shape and size.
I was prevented from seeing these women
Because I've lusted after them in my heart
And other parts of my anatomy all my life long,
So now I was being punished. But I knew
           they were coming,
I could hear their voices sparkle like water,
And I knew there'd be lots of singing.
The one Italian I *could* see—the guy
           with the mustache—
Had already brought the wine. He had
           an accordion, too,
And the women were bringing the food.

Many Italians have river houses
The color of peaches and apricots,
And most are not very large,
Not much more than garden sheds,
But they've all got arbors for dappled shade,
And they sit out there, the Italians,
With their families and friends on their little piazzas,

Eating their pizzas, linguine, and whatnot
Right beside the river, singing and laughing
      their heads off.

Many Italians have river houses, and what
      have we got?
Strip malls. Towns with no trees. Junkyards
      and dumps.
When I think of those lousy Italians, their homemade
      music and fun,
I weep with longing for all that we've lost
      or never possessed.
What's *wrong* with us? Listen, let's go there.
Maybe there are no Italians. Okay.
Maybe those houses don't even exist.
But I know there are rivers.
There always are rivers. Let's go.

In Memoriam: Alex Scornavacco

IV

The Fragrance of
Burning Turf

The Fragrance of Burning Turf

1.

We had seen a Norwegian fjord,
Naked sparrows for sale in Florence,
Hemingway's favorite cafes in France,
But now we had crossed the channel
And landed in Rosslare. The air
Smelled medicinal, smoky sweet:
Fragrance of burning turf.

And then we were gliding away,
Riding the half-empty train,
Pleased by the music of Irish English,
Delighted, relieved, but grave, with students
And duties awaiting us in the West.

The fields were dimming down to brown,
But the hedges still ran green,
And the beaches—or "strands," I suppose
We should say—the strands lay smooth and blonde
With the light blue sea on our right,
And the sea on our right, and the sea
On our right, and the sea on our right
With its light blue light looked absolutely right.

2.

That slight young girl
In a dingy jersey and wool-knit cap,
With a shallow box for coins at her feet,

Her back to the wall in a Galway square,
Howling an old song out of her lungs,
Had a plain flat face and a plain flat voice
But the force of an opera star.
And she was still at it two hours on.

3.

Our driver's name was Michael. While
He would handle the coach, his son
Stephen would manage the transport van
To Galway and return. "I'm bringing him
Into the business. My father's name was Stephen,
Stephen Michael, so Steve Mike. You see?
And I am Michael Stephen or Mike Steve,
As people know me, and my son we call
Steve Mike again. That's the way we like
To go round out here." And all of us laughed.

4.

Through the drifting fog of the passing years,
I only have to squinch my eyes
To see that doll-sized, sharp-toothed shark
Dead on the beach at Inch.

5.

And then descended to Dunquin
After slowly creaking round Slea Head,
The coach and our lives in the balance,
The drop to death just off our left,
The curves right sharp, the asphalt narrow,

Our landboat rocked by lashing wind.
I trapped a shout behind my teeth,
Fingers clenched, the stress tremendous.
But Michael, bless him, banished our anguish,
Easing us down the buffeted heights,
As Great Blasket hove into view,
Abandoned island of the olden ways,
Pale green dragon swimming in seasmoke
With all her islets in tow.

Here was the source of the self-told stories
I loved most—*The Islandman, Twenty Years
A-Growing*, and the woman they called *Peig*.
All three cried out to me like seabirds,
Tantalizing close, but we lacked the time and boat
To reach them except by way of their ghostly words.

> *"We were imbued with the sound of the wind
> that blew in from the seashore,
> beating in our ears every morning,
> clearing our brains and rinsing the dust from our skulls."*

My eyes devoured the view,
But when we departed, I was left
With a longing could not be solved
By fiddle music or song.

6.

A man with rusty, brush-cut hair
Standing by a low stone wall,
His pet fox on a chain.

7.

The moonscape of the Burren came as a shock—
Nothing but rock, we thought—
Limestone, sandstone, mudstone, siltstone
Fractured, slipped, stepped, or swirled into shapes
Like the petrified shells of gigantic snails on their sides.
Nothing but rock from here to the sea, then under the sea,
And breaching way out in the bay, like whales
Rising for air, to appear as the Aran Islands.
Wow. Nothing could live here, we thought,
Nothing but rock—but there was a lonely cow!
And another. And there was a water tank formed,
Of course, from stone. And if we looked more intently,
Bright bands of green that grew from the fissures,
And if we looked more carefully still, there were flowers.
Flowers, for heaven's sake, diminutive pinks and blues,
And others like daisies enlarged, and there, good lord,
If those weren't exquisite orchids!

We stood in a crescent agog in front of a dolmen,
Standing stones with a tablerock roof aslant,
A lean-to temple to honor and guard the dead
From who knew how far back. Slim Tom Flanagan
Had an idea. Scholar of the burren, he stood
Before us, gesturing round, friendly but formal,
Black suit, white shirt, and skinny black tie
Flailing around like the tail of a kite,
Geology, anthropology, botany, history, more
Pouring out of his mouth and flying away in the wind.

8.

A small gray horse
Among gray stones
Grazing in the rain.

9.

Took a solo walk along the coast
Into the village through gathering dark
For the music and dance, and it wouldn't hurt
To cast an eye on our students. Arrived,
And wondered at the white horse
Tied to a tree outside. Inside, a bit of a band,
A bit of a bar, and I ordered my glass of the black.
Dancing was already underway, the place
Already alive. The big surprise was the space
Allowed for whirling, jogging pairs,
No tables, no chairs, the rest of us milling to watch.
That, and the scorching intensity of the light,
Brightened, no doubt, by the whitewashed walls.
Fun: smiles and laughter and twirling bodies,
But something thrummed under the music, too.

A local man spoke the tension for me:
"There's tinkers in town, and some
Of the young ones are here." He nodded at the dance.
"Did you see the horse outside? There could be trouble,
And if it comes, be sure to stand back, make room."

A tune or two later, I heard the word "knife!"
Cut through the din, and the music stopped.

Everyone scrambled, backs to the walls,
Except for the two young men mid-room,
Who circled, then stopped. Words were exchanged
I can't recall, and over the years one of the boys
Just disappeared, but the indignation and hurt
On the face of the boy with wavy brown hair
And a shirt so white in that bright light
It seemed about to combust,
That boy seared my heart and stayed.
I never saw any knife. Friends
Intervened, hauled them apart,
And I heard the man beside me say,
"It's all right so." The music
And dancing resumed.

When I stepped outside, the horse was gone.
Only the odd light shone
Along the coast road home, and so
I walked back gingerly. Now and then,
Other pedestrians passed, and we murmured,
"Good evening" to faces we could not see.
I could hear the waves breaking below,
But the sea was black, the night was large,
And I felt how little I'd ever know.

10.

A leap from the ferry down
Into the curragh to Inishmaan
To front that sandy-haired young man, my age,
Working the long, weathered oars,
His face four feet from mine.

"Fine day," I say. He smiles, answers,
"Aye, but I've seen finer,"
Dragging the ocean behind.

11.

I paid for a cold, small room upstairs
In the house of Bridie O'Connor, who
Also served up hearty meals. Her husband,
On in years, had no English, I no Irish,
So we were *incommunicado,* but
When I asked after the long, faded photograph
Hung on the kitchen wall, depicting a dozen girls
On the beach beneath a cliff, Bridie laughed
And hooked her thumb at her husband,
Where he sat, cloth cap, pipe in hand.
"That's him, him and his friends
When they was small." "But they're all
Wearing dresses!" I protested. "They are,"
Said she. "They're fooling the faeries,
Who always preferred to steal the boys."
She walked straight up to the picture
And pointed with her spoon:
"That's him." And we beamed, all three,
All round, all pleased
The subterfuge succeeded.

12.

After the music on Inishmore,
The priest invited us out of the rain
And ushered us into the priory

For a drink to close out the night.
The chat was vivid and smart. I said,
"It feels like the end of the world
Out here, and I like it." "Next parish,"
He smiled, "America. But there's something
You have to understand. For the people here,"
He said, spreading his arms and hands,
"These islands aren't out, they're in."
I must have looked puzzled. He said,
"You said it feels like the end of the world
Out here, but to them, it's not out, it's in,
And the end of the world's out there—
Rossaveel, Galway, Dublin, New York."

My mind did a somersault, and I saw
In a flash this was true
From the point of view, too,
Of every place on the planet—from
Tierra del Fuego to Gnawbone and Brook,
Kamchatka to Saskatoon,
Home is the center, home is in,
And every place else is out.

13.

Riding the Aran ferry home,
The glitter of the Galway lights
And there on the pier in her navy coat,
My wife in her brand new boots.

14.

Somewhere over by Oughterard,
Driving through the gloaming,
We lugged way down for a little knot
In the traffic flow, and our low beams caught
A young man hoisting a two-pound trout
To show the driver who'd parked his lorry
To gawk and talk. Then we vanished
Into the tunnel our headlights carved,
But the luster of that spotted trout
And the joy in the smiles of those two men
Left an afterglow that has lasted me
For going on half a century.

V

What Happened in
the Museo Sorolla

What Happened in the Museo Sorolla

Madrid was loud with crowds and cars,
But that fresh morning we outwalked
The chaos into quiet neighborhoods
And then the deeper quiet of a stone museum,
Which was once Joaquín Sorolla's house.

We'd never heard of him until, the day before,
He'd caught us at The Prado, stargazing
A canvas six feet long on which he'd left
Three boys stretched out on their bellies
In the shallows of a brown and lilac beach.
They glistened so delightfully those boys
Had driven us to walk these many blocks
To check what might be on the walls
Of this dead painter's house.

The first room held such striking portraits
That we murmured, marveling, but then
Were silenced by *The Mother*, four feet high
And five feet long, mostly bed and wall,
Everything in shades of white except
Two heads resting on puffed pillows:
The mother's, with her mussed black hair,
And, almost lost, a good arm's length away,
The infant's, eyes closed, swaddled in a bonnet.
Otherwise, both bodies had been swallowed
By the billow of the bedding, which was white—

But white of such complexity that it was washed
With pink and blue, warmed with yellow, smudged
With brown, and shaded with some purple, too.
There the mother and her infant lay
Together and apart, honored by their distance
From us, the cumulus in which they were afloat,
Small and vulnerable, exhausted by the long
And messy journey from desire to this birth.

We looked long and long. Then I went on,
Stepping through into the red-walled room
Which had been Sorolla's studio.
The ceilings seemed so high he might have built
A dirigible in there. Indeed, he did not shy
From canvases that could have sailed
A modest boat, choosing, then, to work with
Brushes long as yardsticks. Here were shorter ones,
Heads up, exploding from a vase like a bouquet.

But what froze me in my shoes and soon
Thereafter melted me was the flash and dazzle
Of the sunlit canvases, themselves. These
Were beach paintings: Valencia, where Joaquín
Was orphaned early, raised by relatives,
And to which he kept returning his life long.

I took halting steps around the room
To look, wide-eyed, through these windows
On the seaside scenes that Joaquín loved.

Here, an adolescent, nude but for his broad-
        brimmed hat,
Led his large and naked horse from out the surf,
Both bodies shining wet. There, a girl
In flimsy pink apparel waded on blue sand.
A small bare boy, knee-deep in multicolored
Water, helped his little sailboat sail.
Centered on the end wall, though, in place
Of honor, two women in their summer whites,
With parasol and hat in hand, leaned against the wind,
Skirts and veils and sashes flying back,
More elegant than angels and more real,
Though they were only paint. I knew that.
Didn't I?

    I found myself
Where I'd begun and spun, a slow
Three-sixty, taking in the room, the paintings
Gazing back at me, and felt something
Like water rising in me, but it wasn't
Water, was it, it was light, light,
And Joaquín's love of it, and of his people,
All the colors we are given by this world,
Especially white, plus paint, of course, the squeege
And smear, smidge and dab and sweep of it.
I blurred and overbrimmed so that I could not see
But simply stood there, seared by this surprise,
Then winced and wiped away my tears,
And I've been someone somewhat different
        ever since.

Machado Lives

1.

Antonio Machado, a man
of warmth and strong feeling
but also restraint, most often
appears in black-and-white photos
wearing a suit and tie and,
sometimes, a fedora. Of course,
these were the 1920s and '30s,
but still. You couldn't call him
handsome. His face is reminiscent
of something plain and good:
a potato, maybe,
not at all exotic but
helpful and dependable.
Machado taught French
and took long walks. He
listened to his dreams.
When civil war came, he
ushered his old mother
to safety beyond the Pyrenees,
but both of them died
soon after. Today,
Machado remains
one of Spain's
most beloved poets.

2.
Machado lived simply
in rented rooms most of his life.
In the poor mountain town
where he landed
his first teaching job, Machado
married his landlord's daughter.
Leonor. She was fifteen,
less than half his age. He
loved her deeply. That love
still lives in his poems
a hundred years later. She
died of TB two years after
they married. He grieved
her sorely. That grief
still aches in his poems.

In time, Machado
took a job in Segovia
and a room in a boarding house.
His poems had grown simpler,
like folk songs or the proverbs
of peasants. He did all he could
to return poetry to the people.
Did his poetry speak
so directly because he lived
in such simple rooms?

White inn, he wrote.
The traveler's room,
with my shadow!

Segovia is a fantastic town—
the color of pollen, sand, and gold—
a walled city where Moors left
their mark, with a Roman aqueduct,
with a castle, Alcázar, out on a point
where the land drops away
for hundreds of feet, so you look
far down on treetops.
The castle contains shining armor,
crossbows, spears, and tapestries.
I witnessed all this with my wife
and friends, but what I remember
best are the simple rooms
in the boarding house
where Machado lived.

Climb the stairs
and enter the kitchen, still hung
with the landlady's pans
and utensils over the tile stove.
Down the narrow hall, step up
to the dining room,
where the boarders took
their meals like family.
A small sitting room,
skinny bedroom to one side.
Step through a bigger bedroom,
arriving at last at Machado's place.
Broad-board floor, low ceiling,
iron bed, reading chair,

a round table with books.
Not much more than the cell
of a monk, though Machado
managed a long love affair
with a married woman, so
not such a simple fellow after all.

Machado had to pass through
the bedroom of an old man
in order to reach his own. Those nights
the old man could not sleep
he'd call out to Machado, asking him
for poetry, which Machado would recite
from his own bed
until the old man drifted off.

3.
In the *plaza mayor*
of that city, there stands
a statue that's easy to miss
in all the pedestrian traffic,
a mix of locals and tourists
from all round the world.
It's a bronze, life-size, and so
you're apt to bump into it,
as we did, as if it were only another
person among the people. It's
Machado! He's earthy brown and green.
A scarf drapes off his shoulders,

he's got a cane in hand, and, unlike
most of the statues I've seen,
this one seems about to smile.
We liked him, we liked him a lot.
So my wife and I asked our friends
for a photograph. The sun was bright.
We each looped an arm
around Machado and smiled,
surprised! He was warm.

4.

Once, in America,
in Duluth, Minnesota,
in the 21st Century, in the deep
silence of a Quaker Meeting,
a dark-eyed, dark-haired beauty
who taught Spanish in the schools,
suddenly sang a poem by Machado
to a melody that came to her
like an angel and parted her lips.

In English, the poem goes like this:
  Last night, as I was sleeping,
  I dreamt—marvellous error!—
  that I had a beehive
  here inside my heart.
  And the golden bees
  were making white combs
  and sweet honey

from my old failures.
  Last night, as I slept,
I dreamt—marvellous error!—
that it was God I had
here inside my heart.

  The poem sounds better in Spanish,
of course, and better yet sung
by a dark-eyed, dark-haired beauty·
in a melody so pure it rose
like a dove and dropped in the silence
like a gold coin into a bottomless well
of clear water, and we all
sat stunned, watching it
flash and flash as it fell,
as it tumbled and flashed and fell.

  People were breathing,
people were breathing hard,
as if in great pain, some of them,
and finally the Methodist
preacher who had come
to sit quietly with the Quakers
since he had retired,
whispered, *"Thank you!"*

The Babel of Bilbao

We drove north on the high plateau,
Entered coniferous forests,
Angling upward, flashing past
Whitewashed farms in sunshot meadows,
Then made the long, dramatic run
Downhill steeply toward the sea
As though the Atlantic were magnetic
And drew the steel of our automobile
Relentlessly down to Bilbao.

Bilbao. A hopeless labyrinth for cars.
Somehow we found our hostel, parked,
Napped, and ventured out for a late, late
Lunch on the near empty Plaza Nueva.
We chose our food by pointing: tapas,
Or *pintxos* in the indigenous tongue,
Euskera, a language with two dozen dialects.
We'd arrived at last among the Basques.

A long stroll along the canal, the first
Fallen leaves of autumn crisping
Beneath our feet, light beginning
To leave the day, misty rain
To descend, only to lift as we hustled
With others uphill and turned to cut
Through the Plaza Nueva, then stopped
As if we'd been shot.

The place was packed,
The tables teeming, the high-tops
For two jammed with six, humanity
Standing and spilling every which way—
Glamorous gals and men in their best,
Old gents with crutches or canes,
Great-grannies in wheelchairs,
Babies in arms, kids on the run,
And a living tornado of human talk
Swirling and rising like smoke up a stack.

We'd stumbled into the living room
Of Bilbao, a circus of sound, a furnace
Of noise, and we walked on through,
With me screaming, "This is insane!"

The din was dumbfounding, sublime,
The word "community" incarnate
And gone mad, that flagstone square
The pounding heart of some ancient town
Where inhabitants offered up word
Of their daily wounds and desires
Like pleas to the gods to have mercy
In a roar of Spanish and Euskera.

You could say it was only the sound of a crowd,
And yet I have yet to get over the shock.

Homage to Hondarribia

Who could dislike a town
where an all-weather, outdoor
escalator lets you down
the ridge so you can ride,
gliding like royals,
to step out on stone streets
perfumed by roast meat,
fish boils, flowers, bakery,
and the salt smell of the sea?

Our apartment had no drapery
but pine green shutters
on windows gazing down
where children chased each other.
No extra charge for that, either.
Banners on some balconies
claimed we were not in Spain
but the free republic of Euskadi.

A few too many tourists, like us.
The town, itself, crammed tight
between low mountains and the bay.
But fishing boats left at first light
as they had for centuries,
and there were still fish, by god, thank god.
We ate their delicious flesh
and watched a man with a lengthy rod

haul a sea bass, thrashing, into the mesh
of his net. I see him smiling yet.

Was there always a party in Hondarribia?
Why this band to brighten the day,
galumphing down San Pedro Kalea?
Two trumpets, a tuba, a couple trombones,
silver and brass, blasted a tune,
quit, and the whole damn gang
of women and men exploded in song.
They circled up before a bar,
and we stood tiptoe then to see
a stocky young man in a green beret,
dragging a plastic boat on a rope,
had something important to say,
though what, of course, was a mystery
to the likes of us. "What *is* this?"
one of us asked, and a nearby man
explained, "The rowing club."
As if that answered everything.
The stocky man sang solo now,
and suddenly we were noticing
he was far beyond well endowed
with a ginormous bulge in his pants,
and one young woman slowly bent,
laughing helplessly into her hands.
Had her guy been made club president?
Perhaps he'd won an important race
and this was ritual punishment?
There came a pause, the drum went bang,

and the whole sodality sang.
When we drifted home along toward dark,
that club still sang outside the bars.

Our ears sniffed music in the air
down the kalea the next day, too,
where a pair of strong-voiced, middle-aged men
had drawn a crowd with accordion
and guitar in a sun-bright square.
Locals sang along, and the men
had laid out lyrics there.
Some tourists had the gall to join,
which made me sort of sick. "Look,"
I scoffed, nodding at an Asian woman,
singing with unguarded joy.
"As if," I scoffed, "she understood
the meaning of those words."
But one more chorus, one more verse,
and I was swept out of myself, myself,
singing the nonsense of Euskara,
my voice, too, yanked from the heart,
the same as here, I see with a start,
since I began without one word
but just the wish to sing something
to honor Hondarribia.

Two Balconies: a Mini Mock-Heroic

1.

Our apartment in Logroño
had a balcony, a swallow's nest
stuck to a cliff,
and my wife was out there
sketching rooftops of the city
and the autumn hills beyond,
when I heard her shout and wail.
The wind had snatched
the small sheet from her hand
and sent it sailing like a bird.

I shot through the doorway
and took flight after flight
down and around and down,
down, down, dizzily down
the corkscrew stairs
and out the entrance
to the street. Hopeless:
pedestrians, a few scraps
of trash flapping weakly
in the wind, and yet
halfway up the block
I found her sketch
lying flat, face-down.
I examined it—
nice work!—then climbed

the many steps, turning
and turning, rewinding
myself, with the trophy
in my hand and returned it
to my wife's surprise
and stood there pleased
as a bluebird who'd delivered
an especially attractive banner of grass
to his mate. She went to fetch
her paints, returning
to her perch—but would you
believe it?—a gust grabbed
her sketch, I shot through the door,
repeating our performance, and,
when I returned, sketch in hand,
I told her from now on
she might regard me as a demigod,
He-Who-Defeated-the-Wind.

2.

Walt drove the rolling roads
through vineyards, then on up
the switchbacks through the pines
to the razorback known as El Balcón
de la Rioja. We mounted 280
stone block steps on a zigzag
route through trees,
emerging on a bare rock butte,
about the size of a modest

living room, from which
the view made speech redundant,
although we sighed and cooed
at the expanse below, burnt gold and green,
the crawling vehicles
like beetles, the tiny
towers of the towns.

I'd brought binoculars
around my neck,
a diffident desire in my heart,
but now my wish came true:
I spotted crosses in the sky,
and they kept coming closer,
turned from black
to two-toned buff and chocolate,
and grew into enormous
raptors: Griffon Vultures,
their wingspan wider
than a tall man stands.
We handed the binoculars
around. They filled our glasses.
We told ourselves to watch our feet
and not step off the mountain.
The Griffons rode the lift and loft
of thermals with great grace,
tilting slightly, slipping sideways,
sailing on relentlessly across from us,
below us, coasting down the ridgeline,
hauling the sky behind them like a shawl.

Cheryl turned and told me, "Thank you
for bringing the binoculars." True
gratitude for which I'm truly grateful
to this day, for, though I am a bumbler
by nature, I, too, am glad I bore,
that day, binoculars to El Balcón de la Rioja,
where there be dragons in the sky.

Handpan Song

Prelude

On a bright but biting morning in Madrid,
We hopped off the double-decker
At the Parque del Buen Retiro, the Park
Of the Pleasant Retreat. Just what we needed:
Sun rising and warming. Space. And quiet
Suddenly broken by flocks of large green parakeets
Tearing the air with their screaks and squawks,
Hanging like unripe fruit from the trees,
Foraging the lawn like little old men
Rummaging drawers for mittens.
Parakeets? Hadn't expected *that!*

Song

We walked the avenue beneath tall trees
To the Palacio de Cristal, which, in the end,
Turned out to be an extravagant greenhouse
With few plants but lots of ignorable art.
However, beforehand, we heard faint strains
Of music, then paused beside a few other folks
To listen and watch a somewhat scruffy young man
Beat bell tones out of a metal drum by hand—
Which is to say, with the fingers of both hands
Flickering over a clamshell shape as if
Two gongs had got married or a small
Flying saucer had landed in this boy's lap.
And the music might well have descended from

The Milky Way, for it eddied and streamed, sparkled
And swirled, a song from the other world
That sang of ways of being beyond thought.
It made me feel like champagne, like prayer,
And I could not tear myself away. I tried
Three times to follow my friends, but
Twice I just shuffled off a few steps before
The ethereal music drew me right back.
I offered coins and meant to leave, yet
Could not free myself. At long last,
When the drummer paused for rest, I invented
A gesture of thanks and respect on the spot,
Which the handpan man returned, and I felt,
Finally, free, reluctantly, to go on with my life.

Coda

Home again, I recounted highlights from Spain
For my brother's wife, including how I got caught
By mysterious music in the Parque del Buen Retiro.
I should say that Mary and I are both
Of Swedish extraction, both rather reserved,
And being just a tad proud of my spontaneous
Gesture of thanks to the handpan man,
I thoughtlessly mentioned that. At which,
Mary narrowed her eyes and demanded, "Show me."

Trapped, I made a very slight bow, touched my brow,
Then my heart, then stretched out my open hand.
It is insufficient to say that she laughed. She barked,
She squealed, she gave a couple of donkey honks,

And, though she was seated, bent at the waist
      to beat her legs,
Then wheezed for breath and began again.
Although I was slightly startled at first, I am glad
To report that I joined her without reservation.

VI

The Moon
Beside the Canoe

Island River Redux

Here we go again, on a sweet retreat upriver,
Launching into the great quiet lying in wait all along
And only deepened now by the notable commotion
As a congregation of Canada geese shout their hymn
At our approach: *Rise Up! Rise Up! Rise Up and Go!*

How much of heaven can we ever know?
The cuddle and snuggle and rocking chair,
Ecstatic sex and its afterglow,
The circle of friends round a table,
The liquid passage of our canoe.

Political disaster, family despair
Dissolve in our wake as we go.
Sharp-shins chase the warblers south,
But white water lilies glow on black water,
Calmer than doves or Buddhist nuns.

What grains of wild rice remain
Show yellow, green, and blue maroon,
Reminding us of beads and quills.
They spray and sprinkle our packs as we pass.
Mallards and redheads dabble and dive.

The rice leaves droop like pennants
Of plenty here in this half-drowned land,
Where, long ago, an Ojibwe ancestor dreamed
His band would find food afloat on the water,
And hearing of this, they rose up and went.

Flight

Wandering along the Split Rock River,
Beyond the gravel pits and trails for ATVs,
In golden grass, I nearly stepped on feathers
Where a hunter shucked a grouse, maybe,
Or hungry hawk had found herself a meal.
I bent to look, then turned and walked away
On up the path, where I could hear—or did I feel?—
A ruffed grouse drum...and then the thrum as the covey
Exploded through the trees. That soft thunder
Sent me back to the depression in the grass,
Where I took a knee and gathered several feathers.
Driving home through birch and tamarack,
I laid them on the table for my wife,
Who seemed as pleased as if I'd brought her meat
By these symbols of another, furtive life.
She tied the feathers in a fan, nice and neat,
With blood-red ribbon, a bright contrast
To their soft gray and dark brown bands,
And set them on the windowsill. Feathers last,
And these will often take me out there on the land
While standing in our kitchen, listening and lost.

Bog Root

Bog root, swamp stump, kale root, swede,
So called because commonly eaten
By cold country folk and our creatures—
Long-haired horses, cows, and pigs,
Who are happy enough, snuffling around
In frozen dirt and snowdrifts, to chomp
The cold purple shell of this vegetable
To get at the golden heart of the rutabaga—
That we may survive in our homes
Rather than die on the roads like so many beggars.

Are you sitting fat and sassy in the city?
Are you sipping exotic soups of Asia,
Buzzed on champagne, peppers and spice?
Hard times are coming, winter is coming,
The end of the world is on the way,
And therefore we celebrate bog root
Each year in Askov, Minnesota, the Rutabaga
Capital of the World. In Ithaca, New York,
We hold the International Rutabaga
Curling Championship and play with our food.

The bright spade sunk in black earth
Turns up rutabagas like buried shoes,
The heads of baby dolls we cradle
And carry away to our weathered sheds.
We skin them, we cut them in cubes

To simmer in soups and stews.
We mash them with carrots and spuds
And heap them in hills on our plates,
Anointed with butter, while cracks
Quickfracture the frozen lakes,
Booming like thunder. Inside, we're warm,
Thanks to bog root. We savor its tang
On the tongue, the tincture of cyanide
In the mellow mash by means of which we survive.

And so, while the well and all hell
Freeze over, as the bombs whistle down,
While the trees along the horizon
Explode into flame, come join with me, children,
Say: Give us this day our daily bog root.

Skyfall

Down the dusky glimmer of dawn,
snowfluff falls like ash
or stuffing come out of clouds,
or a heavy downdrift of cottonwood seeds,
milk froth, sea foam, a softness aloft,
almost appalling in dreamy descent,
ghosting the rooftops and trees,
yet lovely in lazy surrender and sift,
the gentle shock of an eyeful of skyfall
insisting we're lucky to live
where water can blossom in air
and our walkways fill
with infinitesimal flowers,
though the need to lift
and shift these dazzling drifts
is apt to put an ache in the back
it may take days to cure.

A Visitation

I'm sick of being sick. Sick sucks.
My gut's been grinding for weeks
With a few reprieves when the pills
Banged the bad bugs. Pow!
For a while there, I felt okay
And learned again how that's a lie:
Okay is not okay. Okay is good.
Feel bad for long enough, okay seems mighty good,
While good looks great, and great's a state
We don't deserve except to visit,
Maybe, like Vermont. Anyway,
I'm going to the bathroom now,
But stay right here 'cause I'll be back.

As I was saying, sickness sucks,
In part because it separates you from your body.
Ever notice that? Here you thought your body
Was your buddy, but suddenly he's gone,
Gone over to the other side, and up
And whacked you, whoever *you* are. Are you
Anyone at all once your body's gone?
Or it's like some broke-down dog
So needy you can't leave the house because
You've got this history, you owe her,
Plus, you own her, though now it seems

The other way round. There's a mind-body
Problem here somewhere, but I'm too sick
To say just what.
      However,
I *can* still complain. I've been doing that for weeks.
We're good at that, aren't we? I should know.
An expert, I used to sit in bars at midnight
And listen to the whining rising through the smoke:
My boss, my mom, my useless roommate. Ish.
My job, my class, my crappy car, my rotten life.
The moan, the sob, the righteous rant. My god,
It was horrifying—and all too much like me.
Homo sapiens, my ass. *Homo complainus,*
Of which I am a prime example, so I won't.

Except to say one final time that sickness sucks,
And I was stuck in it this afternoon when I stepped out
A moment for the mail, and there, in the yard
In the snow by the low stone wall
Stood a six-point buck in his dark fall coat,
Proud and unafraid, who held me with his look,
His mesmerizing eyes, his pure white throat.
Here was health on the hoof. I muttered
Admiration as I drifted toward this prince
Of the rut, who stood just a short shot away.
He spooked and jumped the wall but then
Delicately high-stepped to a patch

Of last grass and lowered his body,
His beautiful body, beneath the blessing arms
Of a deep green spruce.

      Was this a sign,
I wondered, or just a handsome deer
Who happened by our place?
And I said, "Yes."

The Winter Vixen

Glancing through the glazed window,
I saw a fox, strawberry blonde,
Hunting among the white windrows.
Charmed by her neat black stocking-feet
As she rummaged below the bare lilacs,
I dropped what I was working on,
Curious what she'd find to eat.
Then I saw the second fox,
Half her size, hesitant, downright darling.
Could Mother find food for more than one?
The vixen nosed a stiffened starling
Out of a drift and crunched it down.
Frozen in place, I watched them go,
Padding over the crusted snow.

Redpoll Ruckus

Little Flitter, Finch of Winter,
Welcome to my thistle seeds.
Feed, my flighty friend,
Fulfill your thin, small self.
I like your black chin,
Your snub-nose bill,
Your brown offset
By the blush on your breast,
Not to mention, of course,
The raspberry dab
You wear as your crown.

Here you come, bang, in a bunch,
Looking for lunch, a handful
Flung in a flock, to glean
The ground beneath the weeds,
Or, one by one, you will
Cling to the feeder and eat
Seed after seed after seed.
Good grief! What greed!
Who knows what you need
To weather such crackling cold?
We'll weather this weather together.

A Beaver Lodge

I took the bridge and hiked uphill
Across the dreary clear-cut, then on
Through spruce where water spilled
And trickled from the beaver pond.

Climbing up the waist-high dam,
I watched the silver surface wink
With insect life. Mallards swam
In peace. I teetered on the brink

And cast a feathered spinnerbait
Among the trunks of naked trees.
I'd come too early or too late.
All I offered failed to please.

But how about those dimples there,
Just off that distant, sedgy point
Where beavers had their rustic lair?
I worked my way around the pond

In hopes of catching speckled trout—
Mucky footing, boughs to dodge,
Mosquitoes in their rising clouds—
Until I stood beside the lodge.

What a hodgepodge house to own!
As if a fright-wig eagle's nest

Had fallen here, but upside down.
Yet it had stood the winter's test.

And then I heard a gnawing sound,
The whimper of a beaver kit,
And grown-ups grumbling underground
So that I lost or found my wits

And stood there listening, stunned and dumb,
Absorbed by what I can't forget,
This life beyond my paltry one—
Thriving, secret, intimate.

The Jacks

You've heard about the lumber camps,
   Where the jacks were worked like mules.
Breakfast wolfed by oil lamps,
   According to the rules:
"No talking! You want more cakes,
   Just point." Then off to the cut
To whack and saw till muscles ached
   And drooping eyelids shut.
Friday nights, they hit the Shore
   To burn straight through their pay
On drink and cards, a hare-lipped whore,
   And brawling through two days.
Poor brutes. In less than four decades,
   They slaughtered the virgin trees,
Bequeathing us their dunderheaded
   Blind rapacity.

White Feather

I'm paddling upriver, upwind,
When the water widens like a lake,
The blue deepens, the wind stiffens,
I have to dig and strain. It's work,
But I'm glad enough to bend to the task and forget,
For now, my daughter's blast of acrid anger
From ten days back, which pursues me
The way smoke follows you round a fire.

This country got smoked right down to rock
Some time ago—jack pines torched, cedars
Scorched to skeletons along the banks—
So it bucks me up to see young aspens sprung
As tall as I can stretch and jack pines shoulder-high.

Up ahead, a white fleck rides the blue,
And as we pass, I see the fleck is one down feather,
Quill erect, a miniature mast, the feather curved
Like a spinnaker taut with wind. I want to shout
"Ahoy there, mate!" but I'm groaning against a gust,
And the little white sailboat's gone.

No walleyes at the rapids, but the firestorm
Spared the portage, a green oasis in this bone yard,
And I lunch in the fragrant shade of seasoned cedars.
Quickened by rest, carried by current, nudged along
By the breeze at my back, I'm relaxed on my return—

And amazed, a mile downriver, to sight *White Feather*
Not just afloat but faring along quite nicely, thanks.

To the sailor who steers *White Feather*,
So small he can't be seen, my canoe
Must resemble a trireme, gigantic, titanic,
And yet *White Feather* sails steadily on,
And I think of the Vikings sailing blind
For Vinland, of Mandans in their bullboats
Down the Swirling Waters, of Brendan in his coracle,
His willingness to be blown wherever
God seemed to want him to go,
Of Wynken, Blynken, and Nod
Out fishing among the stars.

And how bungling through a midlife crackup
Feels like shooting a deadly rapids
With little to no control, but somehow
Most people survive. Oh, I know
White Feather is only an accident
Of happenstance. The forces of physics apply.
Sooner or later, the downy wee sloop will sink.
And yet as I pass *White Feather*, I memorize
Her image as a motto for emergencies,
For keeping my wits and hope together,
By telling myself, beneath my breath:
"White Feather, White Feather."

Ghosts

How long ago did I step out
On that flat rock by the boggy bank
To take a break and pull the canoe
Up snug, out of the current?
It was early spring, the water cold.
I arched my back, let go a groan,
And smiled. No one around for miles.

But there was a flash, and another,
Back in the cedars. On a hunch and a hope,
I gave a soft whistle. I whistled,
And, lo, he showed, with, first,
A pale face in the cedar fronds,
And then, caving to curiosity,
Exposed himself with a swoop
To a bush in the bog: a gray jay,
Like a chickadee big as a robin.

Unlike their raucous cousins, the blues,
The grays keep still. If they call at all,
It's apt to be chatters and clicks
Or soft whistles. They resemble
Stuffed toys you wish you could
Offer some kids, but they're ghostly,
Arriving in silence, and often
Departing the same.

I confess I was foolishly proud and glad
To have whistled this one out of the woods,
And I loved the smooth of his swoop from one bush
To the next till he perched on the branch
Of a snag nearby and cocked his head
To consider me.

This jay was on his own but
Brought me flocks of memories
Of his kind in winter camps
Where I sat with friends on balsam boughs
Round crackling fires of cedar and spruce—
Not to mention the black-and-white
Photograph on the wall of my study
Of Joe, my ruddy-faced friend
Who shot himself dead in his thirties
But looks happy there in his twenties,
Standing before his snow-capped cabin
Many long miles north of nowhere,
Arm stretched out like a falconer's
And a gray jay perched on his hand.

This one gave me one last look and was gone.
I settled in the canoe and also moved along.
We left behind a low flat rock in the river
And a snag with a lone bare branch.

Catching Crappies Beneath a Pictograph

No walleyes yesterday, none so far today,
He trolls the river mindlessly, drinking in
The silence like a whisky called Serenity.
His paddle drips. The white-throats call.

How long since he's been back in here?
Eight years? Too long, god knows, too long.
And how far to the pictograph?
Just that much farther than he thought.

But now a whale of granite breaches
Bankside on the right, rising
Out of boggy ground. He slows
And drifts beneath the cliff,

Searching till it startles him.
Oh, yes. Hello. Figures on the rockface,
Facing him full-on, a man with something
In his hand—a knife, a club, a bow?

An antlered buck beside him, also
Facing out, and smaller, lower left,
A raven looking west. Such images
Have stuck to rock for centuries,

Painted by Ojibwe or the ones
Who came before. Iron oxide,
Mixed with fish oil, daubed on stone.
But how did they climb up so high—

Fifteen, twenty feet—to paint?
Sheer wall, the river right below.
Winter work? Just snowshoe up
A drift packed in against the cliff?

What's this? His rod is bowed
And pulsing at his thigh like blood
That surges in his heart. He snatches up
The handle, yanks, reels against

Resistance, there's a leap and splash,
And he shouts "Bass!" He reels again
Against the dodging, diving fish,
Says, "Let me land him, Grandma."

And he does, he nets it, lifts. The fish
Explodes, baptizing him with waterdrops.
The man sits back, surprised,
And says its name: "A crappie? Crappie!"

The fish is a good foot long,
Oversized, glistening emerald, gold,
But better than treasure out here:
It can be eaten: Delectable flesh.

This beauty tied to a stringer,
The stringer to his canoe, he casts again
With a trembling hand. Two days out,
Time and the land are absorbing him.

The white man thanks his grandmother.
His feelings swim and soar.
He gazes at the pictograph.
He catches four fish more.

Several Sorts of Dawn

A chip, a chirp, a hesitant but buzzy chir.
Something like a question speaking without words.
A sense of darkness lifting, very, very slow.
A momentary doubt about this path and where it goes.
A brightening, a listening, a whistle, what was that?
A lowering yourself nearby but where you've never sat.
A light pink wash that, gradually, deepens into rose.
A shameful thought, you've said it, now everybody knows.
The fog, retreating, leaves a dew-drenched web.
Whatever you believed in seeming somehow off instead.
It's early yet. No sun as such. You couldn't call it day.
A liking for a stranger, but it's still too soon to say.

Swansong

Does it make any sense at all
To mention the soul on a day like today,
The lake deep silver, the sky a foggy gray,
Drizzle drifting through in waves,
And a single silver trout
Rattling the willow of my creel
As he suffocates for me? It's cold.
And quiet, the songbirds gone south,
Except for the *roik, roik* of a raven,
Followed by some trumpeting and thunder
As five swans at the far end of the lake
Decide, altogether, to get up and go.
I see the swans, like Jesus, can walk on water
As long as they keep running really hard,
Their wide wings colliding as they beat, beat, beat,
Beat and rise, and something lifts inside me
As they pass, shining like a snowstorm,
Laboring but taking flight.

The Moon Beside the Canoe

The full moon floats like a water lily
Beside the bow of the beached canoe.
I saw this years and years ago
With a friend who showed me through
This country, dead for decades now.
Back then, there were dozens of lakes to explore
And mysteries galore: Was God for real?
Was love? Could I make some words stand still?

I've seen the moon afloat like this
A hundred times since then.
I've seen my words pressed into books
Like keepsakes left behind. I've married
Twice, raised another man's kids,
And sometimes wondered why.
The wind blows where it will;
There's little we truly control.
No need to travel far these days:
A pond will float the moon.

I never met God, though I heard voices
In the wind and smelled perfume
In stands of balm of Gilead.
Strange feelings came to me at dawn
And dusk, but I learned to make do
With friends and a woman's touch.
I put my faith in granite and spruce
And the moon beside the canoe.

VII

Coda

Here

The paddles dip at a steady clip;
   You can hear them hiss and drip.
The fog feels close, and as we go,
   All sounds sound soft and low.
We travel here with love and fear
   In a place that we revere,
Feeling most at home when we're alone
   Where loons and owls both moan.
Should we take a break? Let's try to make
   The far end of the lake,
Though it's hard to see through the mystery
   A single rock or tree.
We squint and peer. I'm glad we're here.
   I believe it's going to clear.

Acknowledgments

I am grateful to the editors of the following magazines and anthologies in which some of these poems, or earlier versions of them, first appeared.

Blueline: "Island River Redux," "Swansong"

California Quarterly: "The Kelp at San Simeon"

Home: an Anthology of Minnesota Fiction, Memoir, and Poetry: "Beds for the Homeless"

Innisfree Poetry Journal: "Bog Root"

Le Spectre: "Firearms and Backhoe"

Lost Lake Folk Opera: "Lost Locations"

Nodin Poetry Anthology: "After Forty Years, Steve Luxton, Poet of the Eastern Townships, Comes to Visit, and We Talk Nonstop for Days," "Big Ideas"

Pensive Journal: "The Baba Way"

Poems of Hope and Resistance: "Good to Have a Brother," "Here," "Several Sorts of Dawn"

The Road Not Taken: "Why Swedes are So Stiff"

Tar River Poetry: "Thea Sofia Beneath the Piano"

Thunderbird Review: "A Beaver Lodge," "Daylilies," "Flight"

Valparaiso Poetry Review: "White Feather"

Wild Goose Poetry Review: "Marsh Marigolds"

Twelve lines from page 43 and 3 lines from page 137 from *Times Alone: Selected Poems of Antonio Machado* © 1983 by Antonio Machado translated by Robert Bly. Published by Wesleyan University Press. Used by permission.

Several of the poems in this collection were broadcast over public radio stations KURU, Silver City, New Mexico, and WTIP, Grand Marais, Minnesota. My gratitude to their producers, with special thanks to Jamie Newton at KURU. The first form of publication for "Louise" was a broadcast by Patrick Hicks on *Poetry from Studio 47* over South Dakota Public Broadcasting.

I owe continuing gratitude to family and friends. Among those not named in the poems, Jim Johnson, Jim Lenfestey, Ilze Mueller, Howard Nelson, Dave and Nancy Pearson, Jean Replinger, Doran and Jane Whitledge, and Pat and Laurie Wilson offered many forms of criticism and inspiration. Jim Johnson, Mark Sunwall, and Jean Turbes were especially helpful with "Three Big Rocks." Years after writing "I'd Like to Sleep Like the Seals on the Beach at Point Lobos," I realized that its title, which also serves as its first line, bears more than a little family resemblance to the title of song lyrics by Michael Dennis Browne, "I'd Like to Sleep Like the Pigs at the State Fair," which I'd long admired. Thank you, Michael.

And my gratitude goes, again, to Norton Stillman and John Toren of Nodin Press, for welcoming this collection and ushering it into print with care.

Bart Sutter

June 2022

About the Author

Bart Sutter received the Minnesota Book Award for poetry with *The Book of Names: New and Selected Poems*, for fiction with *My Father's War and Other Stories*, and for creative non-fiction with *Cold Comfort: Life at the Top of the Map*. Among other honors, he has won a Jerome Foundation Travel & Study Grant (Sweden), a Loft-McKnight Award, and the Bassine Citation from the Academy of American Poets. In 2006, he was named the first Poet Laureate of Duluth. He has written for public radio, he has had four verse plays produced, and he often performs as one half of The Sutter Brothers, a poetry-and-music duo. Bart Sutter lives on a hillside overlooking Lake Superior with his wife, Dorothea Diver.